This Little Piggy Went Marketing

9 Simple & Easy Marketing Concepts
For Effectively Increasing Your Impact & Income

Alicia "WATERS"

Copyright © 2014 Alicia "WATERS"

All rights reserved. Except for use in the case of brief quotations embodied in critical articles and reviews, the reproduction or utilization of this work in whole or part in any form by any electronic, digital, mechanical or other means, now known or hereafter invented, including xerography, photocopying, scanning, recording, or any information storage or retrieval system, is forbidden without prior written permission of the author and publisher.

The scanning, uploading, and distribution of this book via the Internet or via any other means without permission of the publisher and author is illegal and punishable by law. Purchase only authorized versions of this book and do not participate in or encourage electronic piracy of copyrighted materials. Your support of the author's rights is appreciated.

Names, characters, places, and incidents are based on the author's own personal experience therefore names of persons and entities remain unnamed to protect the integrity of the story and the privacy of those involved. Any group or organization listed is for informational purposes only and does not imply endorsement or support of their activities or organization.
For ordering, booking, permission, or questions, contact the author.

www.anwempires@gmail.com

ISBN-13:978-1494999292

ISBN-10:1494999293

Printed in the United States of America by Create Space

This Little Piggy Went Marketing

Dedication & Acknowledgment

This book is a general dedication to all who are on the journey of achieving effective marketing solutions in their entrepreneurial endeavors.

I give thanks and acknowledgments to God and all who have enriched my marketing efforts.

Table of Contents

Introduction

Considered Keeping a Marketing Journal

Try A Nonlinear Approach to Marketing

Choose to Have It Your Way When It Comes to Marketing

The Importance of Creating Marketable Content

Increase Your Marketing Efforts Through Bloggertizing

5 Minute Marketing: Effective Marketing Using Less Time

Explore Entireweb As a Marketing Option

Learn How to Become a Great Content Marketer with Audience Bloom

Advance Your Marketing Efforts Hosting a Weekly Mini-Radio Tips Show

Conclusion
Marketing Journal Planner

This Little Piggy Went Marketing

Introduction

Making daily decisions about best marketing practices can be challenging at times especially if you have already spent much of your time and resources trying to accomplish your marketing efforts.

This Little Piggy Went Marketing is a mini handbook guide created from my blog posts with concepts that aid and assist with aligning your marketing efforts for making wise investments of time and money.

The primary goal of marketing your business or products is to be able to monetize your efforts through marketing while changing the lives of others through your offerings.

The overall concept of *This Little Piggy Went Marketing* is about being an intuitive marketer who partners with the energy of your bank account to allow your piggy bank to provide you with insights about your marketing agenda.

These insights will help you to monetize your marketing from an intuitive and metaphysical vantage point.

This guide and journal planner is designed to inspired you to take your marketing efforts to the next level through creating more structure and success.

Incorporating these tips into your marketing efforts will help to increase your impact and your income.

This Little Piggy Went Marketing

Considered Keeping a Marketing Journal

Have you ever considered keeping a marketing journal? I've incorporated a journal into my marketing efforts to enhance my overall success.

Having a specific place for all of your marketing thoughts is a very powerful way to keep focus and create structure. This allows you to formulate a plan to incorporate into your business agenda immediately or at another time.

Call to Action:

If you haven't tried keeping a marketing journal, give it a try and see if it will create a better flow in your framework.

Use the journal and planning pages in the back of this resource to help you get started.

Try A Nonlinear Approach to Marketing

When it comes to the subject of marketing, I've found over the years that is not about always following a simple step by step formula or linear format to bring the results that you desire.

Sometimes you have to try a nonlinear approach and use your marketing efforts in a completely different way. In Luke 19:30 New American Standard Version 1977 it says; "Go into the village opposite *you,* in which as you enter you will find a colt tied, on which no one yet has ever sat; untie it and bring it *here.*"

Sometimes you have to go and market in an arena that you've never considered. It's called cross-marketing or sub-niche marketing. This is where you expand outside of your normal target audience to add value in new territories, gain more exposure and do something different than what is being done by other so called experts.

Call to Action:

Take some time to connect intuitively with your inner money wisdom to discover or explore nonlinear ways to market more effectively.

Choose to Have It Your Way When It Comes To Marketing

Sometimes you have to consciously choose to have it your way when it comes to creating your marketing agenda. I've tried several marketing strategies in the past, honestly, I just don't think that there are any one size fits all when it comes to anything and especially marketing. So, I challenged myself to live by the Burger King slogan of "Have It Your Way."

Often, those who teach marketing will try to provide you with a cookie cut success formula for you to model after in your own way. However, most of the system won't work for many because we each have a different marketing DNA.

So, how do you have it your way? You have it your way by examining what is on the marketing menu of strategies that have been presented to you. Next, you ask for divine guidance on what you should keep, eliminate and how to formulate your success factor based on your discoveries.

After you begin to try that on for size record your journey, assess and keep creating more organization and alignment to help you become more consistent.

This Little Piggy Went Marketing

Call to Action:

This week try having it your way when it comes to your marketing efforts. At first, it might seem like you're a little all over the place, however, the more you do it, you will discover your unique process to continue masterfully marketing your way.

The Importance of Creating Marketable Content

I've been spending quite a bit of time lately learning more about creating marketable content. It's vitally important to learn what and how to say what really matters as it relates to the value that you are here to add to the lives of others.

I recently attended a webinar that was hosted by million-dollar marketing coach, Kendall Summerhawk on that topic. Kendall asks the important question to her audience; Is your content marketable?

Bill Gates says; "Content Is King." This is why it is so important to begin creating nothing less than marketable content for your target market.

Call to Action:

Visit: http://kendallsummerhawk.com/is-your-content-marketable-2/ to learn more about marketable content creation.

Next, make a plan and do more research on marketable content to find more information that will be aligned with your marketing agenda.

Increase Your Marketing Efforts Through Bloggertizing

Often, many entrepreneurs have a challenging time with self-promotion for advertising their brands effectively. There have been many myths about how we should market. Old paradigm techniques that are no longer relevant to the marketing needs of today continue to keeps us stuck.

Though there are many effective methods for marketing and advertising, I don't feel that any one formula or method is always going to be a one size fits all for your platforms DNA. Nor do I feel that every marketing/advertising plan has to be a long or hard process.

There are several creative avenues for advertising effectively, ways that will help you not only leverage your time but also generate the leads and income that you desire.

One effective way to achieve quantum success in your advertising is through using a mini-process of what I call **BLOGGERTIZING.**

BLOGGERTIZING is a concept of using your blog posts as short ads to empower your readers, add value and provide a call to action that leads them to your product or services.

Call to Action:

Look at taking your marketing and advertising efforts to a new level through creating a blog post to add value to your clients and prospect in simple easy steps. Provide a solution for their main challenges.

Create a lead-in to your product or services to help them create a plan of action for accountability and consistency towards their forward movement.

These key steps should help you to get started on your **BLOGGERTIZING** journey.

5 Minute Marketing:
Effective Marketing Using Less Time

Marketing doesn't always have to involve using up a lot of your time in order to be effective. Though marketing has to be consistent, there are ways to leverage your time to achieve your online marketing goals by having the right systems in place.

I came across Brain Moran's, plan for *5 Minute Marketing*, which helps entrepreneurs achieve their marketing goals in very simplistic ways. Concepts that helps you to leverage your time along with reaching your financial goals.

I subscribed to their list and I watched a video called the *Freedom Formula*. This video shows you how to set up an online marketing strategy with everything from how to build your list, enroll people to get your products and programs and so much more in 5 minutes or less.

Call to Action:

Check out the video and other resources from **www.5minutemarketing.com** and see if it's a great fit for your marketing endeavors.

Explore Entireweb As a Marketing Option

I discovered a resource for marketing that I'm currently trying out called Entireweb. This is a free submission search engine that finds and returns relevant websites, images and real time results.

Entireweb's primary goal is to be a leading supplier of search technology solutions. If you haven't already explored this option, then I invite you to consider giving it a try to advance your marketing efforts.

Call to Action:

Explore **www.entireweb.com** to advance your marketing efforts.

Learn How to Become
A Great Content Marketer with Audience Bloom

I was feeling kind of stuck around my marketing efforts one day, wondering what my next steps would be for doing some advertising. I'm an avid learner so I'm always interested to know what would be a great educational tool for discovering how to market more effectively.

I asked myself the question, what should I do when I don't know what I should do about marketing? So, I actually typed that question in the search engine and *Audience Bloom* was one of the options that came up.

Audience Bloom's primary focus is on content marketing that grows your audience. Being the marketing explorer that I am, I checked it out and came across a free downloadable resource called, *The Definitive Guide to Marketing Your Business Online*.

Call to Action:

Consider spending some time over the next few weeks learning more marketing strategies from this resource. I encourage you to explore their website and allow it to add value to your marketing efforts.

This Little Piggy Went Marketing

Advance Your Marketing Efforts
Hosting a Weekly Mini-Radio Tips Show

One of the best ways to achieve your viral marketing efforts for reaching your target audience is through using internet radio platforms. If your goal is to get more exposure for your brand or services, then choosing the right online radio platform can assist you with global advertising.

One way that you can leverage your time effectively is by hosting a 5 to 15-minute tip show where you can share tips from your area of expertise. Using some of your current materials from your blogs, published books or even programs that you've created can be a great way to add value or create lead-ins to your services.

BlogTalkRadio is a great platform to use in this endeavor. They have several different accounts to suit your radio advertising needs. Since I'm suggesting doing mini-tip shows, using their free account would be most recommended. The free account allows you to schedule a 15 to 30-minute show daily.

Also, BTR provides an online university for learning how to effectively market and monetize your show. Incorporating mini-shows into your marketing plan a few times a week is a great way for adding value to others while providing your infomercial as well.

People need what you have to offer and now is the time to share your gifts, change lives and monetize your efforts.

Call to Action:

Consider hosting a mini-tips show online to increase your marketing impact.

If you already host a show online, consider possibly revamping it into a tip show or adding an additional show where you offer tips only.

Conclusion

No matter how successful we've been in our business agendas up to this point, there will be times when we're faced with making numerous decisions big or small. Often, business owners fret over whether they are making the right decisions or choosing the right path especially as it relates to marketing.

It is hard for us to effectively get into our game of marketing and play at the highest level, if we aren't sure about trusting ourselves enough to make the right moves. I feel that we should step out to explore, trust our process, and course-correct if needed.

Like in the game of chess, the pieces each have their specific function along with being strategically positioned to make their right moves at the right time. Chess players understand that they have to be in deep connectedness with the game in order to make the right moves of correctly positioning their pieces at the right time.

Because we are each powerful enough to set up our marketing games, we can correctly position our plans using our intuition and create right inspired actions to proceed moving forward with absolute certainty.

As long as we allow our intuition to guide us in our marketing decision-making process, we will not be lead astray from our path of true purpose and prosperity. We will always make the right moves that are aligned for our greater marketing success.

Set up in your marketing game today by learning how to become more intuitive. Spend some quiet time being still each day connecting to your inner knowing. The results of our inner nudging become powerful manifestations in our marketing efforts.

Marketing Journal/Planner

This Little Piggy Went Marketing

Marketing Journal Questions

How do I feel about marketing right now?

What are the reasons for these feelings?

This Little Piggy Went Marketing

What would I like to change or experience different about my marketing?

What are my next steps?

This Little Piggy Went Marketing

What am I currently learning?

What am I curious to know?

This Little Piggy Went Marketing

Reflections & Actions
(Record insights from the reading or journaling to create a plan)

This Little Piggy Went Marketing

More Notes:

Marketing Journal Questions

How do I feel about marketing right now?

What are the reasons for these feelings?

This Little Piggy Went Marketing

What would I like to change or experience different about my marketing?

What are my next steps?

This Little Piggy Went Marketing

What am I currently learning?

What am I curious to know?

This Little Piggy Went Marketing

Reflections & Actions
(Record insights from the reading or journaling to create a plan)

This Little Piggy Went Marketing

More Notes:

Marketing Journal Questions

How do I feel about marketing right now?

What are the reasons for these feelings?

What would I like to change or experience different about my marketing?

What are my next steps?

This Little Piggy Went Marketing

What am I currently learning?

What am I curious to know?

This Little Piggy Went Marketing

Reflections & Actions
(Record insights from the reading or journaling to create a plan)

More Notes:

Marketing Journal Questions

How do I feel about marketing right now?

What are the reasons for these feelings?

This Little Piggy Went Marketing

What would I like to change or experience different about my marketing?

What are my next steps?

This Little Piggy Went Marketing

What am I currently learning?

What am I curious to know?

This Little Piggy Went Marketing

Reflections & Actions
(Record insights from the reading or journaling to create a plan)

This Little Piggy Went Marketing

More Notes:

Marketing Journal Questions

How do I feel about marketing right now?

What are the reasons for these feelings?

This Little Piggy Went Marketing

What would I like to change or experience different about my marketing?

What are my next steps?

This Little Piggy Went Marketing

What am I currently learning?

What am I curious to know?

This Little Piggy Went Marketing

Reflections & Actions
(Record insights from the reading or journaling to create a plan)

More Notes:

Marketing Journal Questions

How do I feel about marketing right now?

What are the reasons for these feelings?

This Little Piggy Went Marketing

What would I like to change or experience different about my marketing?

What are my next steps?

This Little Piggy Went Marketing

What am I currently learning?

What am I curious to know?

This Little Piggy Went Marketing

Reflections & Actions
(Record insights from the reading or journaling to create a plan)

More Notes:

Marketing Journal Questions

How do I feel about marketing right now?

What are the reasons for these feelings?

What would I like to change or experience different about my marketing?

What are my next steps?

This Little Piggy Went Marketing

What am I currently learning?

What am I curious to know?

This Little Piggy Went Marketing

Reflections & Actions
(Record insights from the reading or journaling to create a plan)

More Notes:

Marketing Journal Questions

How do I feel about marketing right now?

What are the reason for these feelings?

This Little Piggy Went Marketing

What would I like to change or experience different about my marketing?

What are my next steps?

This Little Piggy Went Marketing

What am I currently learning?

What am I curious to know?

This Little Piggy Went Marketing

Reflections & Actions
(Record insights from the reading or journaling to create a plan)

This Little Piggy Went Marketing

More Notes:

Marketing Journal Questions

How do I feel about marketing right now?

What are the reasons for these feelings?

This Little Piggy Went Marketing

What would I like to change or experience different about my marketing?

What are my next steps?

This Little Piggy Went Marketing

What am I currently learning?

What am I curious to know?

This Little Piggy Went Marketing

Reflections & Actions
(Record insights from the reading or journaling to create a plan)

More Notes:

Write A Brief Summary Of Your Marketing Planning Experience

Summary Continued:

Other Related Books on Amazon

Feed the Right Piggy Bank
Feed The "Write" Piggy Bank
I Like Frog Legs & Ham
Fattening Your Piggy Bank
Profitable Aha Moments
Creating Profitable Piggy Banks

This Little Piggy Went Marketing

For More Resources

Visit:

www.marketingmasterymarketplace.blogspot.com

www.profitablepiggybankspower.blogspot.com

www.amazon.com/author/alicianwaters

Or

To Book the Author

For Speaking Engagements

Email: www.anwempires@gmail.com

If you enjoyed this resource, please consider writing a review on Amazon.com.

Thanks & Blessings!

www.ingramcontent.com/pod-product-compliance
Lightning Source LLC
Chambersburg PA
CBHW071805170526
45167CB00003B/1179